What If Dinosaurs Lived Today?

by Mrs. Bauman's class
with Tony Stead

capstone

All Kinds of Dinosaurs

Scientists think that dinosaurs lived between 230 million and 65 million years ago before they became extinct. The climate was very different then! Earth was covered with deserts and hot, wet forests. Could dinosaurs live today? Let's find out more about different kinds of dinosaurs before we answer that question!

Long-necked Plant Eaters

by Omar and Jumana

Apatosaurus was a type of long-necked dinosaur. It was very big, about 75 feet long. Its feet were like elephants' feet. It had a very strong tail. When enemies came close, it may have used its tail like a whip to defend itself.

Apatosaurus lived in herds. It laid eggs as big as soccer balls. Apatosaurus was also a herbivore. That means it was a plant eater. It reached down to eat plants and ferns from the ground. It may have eaten leaves from trees, too. Apatosaurus ate bit by bit, mostly all day long, because its jaws were small.

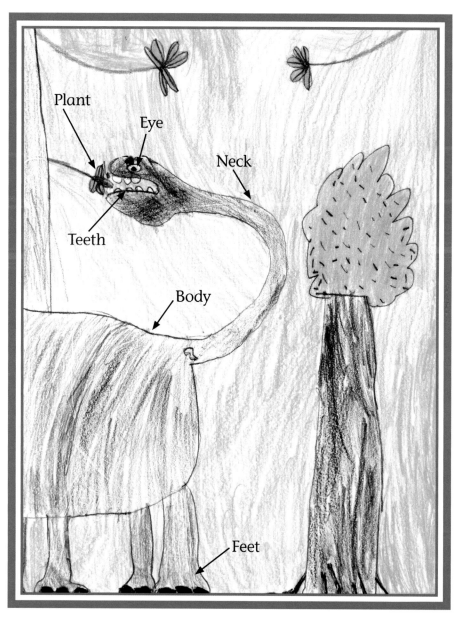

illustrated by Olivia and Ruth

Armored Dinosaurs

by Jack, Victoria, and William

Some dinosaurs had tough bony skin, like armor. Most bony-skinned dinosaurs were herbivores. Their thick skin helped protect them from meat-eating predators. Ankylosaurus also had a big club on the end of its tail. It could hit predators with it.

Some dinosaurs like Stegosaurus had spikes and plates on their backs to help defend themselves.

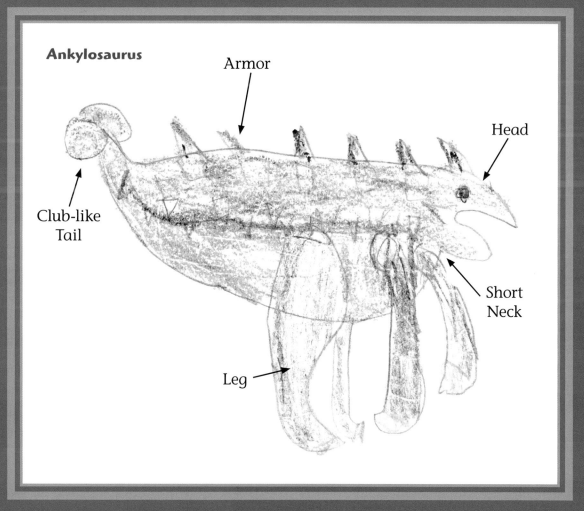

Ankylosaurus

Armor

Head

Club-like
Tail

Short
Neck

Leg

illustrated by Prakruti

Horned Dinosaurs

by Aditya, Jackie, and Shafia

Triceratops was a horned dinosaur. It was strong and big. It had three horns on its head. Triceratops was a herbivore like Apatosaurus. It used its horns to fight off other dinosaurs. It had a long, beaked mouth for chopping and eating plants.

Triceratops had a shield-shaped bone at the back of its head. This neck frill kept its head and neck safe from meat-eating predators.

Fun Fact

Triceratops means "three-horned face."

Fast Hunters

by Agastya and Akein

Velociraptor was a small but powerful meat-eating dinosaur. It lived in desert areas. The name Velociraptor means "speedy thief." Velociraptor liked to eat lizards and other small reptiles. It also hunted in packs to kill much bigger dinosaurs.

Velociraptor had serrated teeth. It also had curved claws on its feet. The claws helped it to climb up trees and cling on to prey.

Fun Fact

Velociraptor stood on two feet and could jump really high!

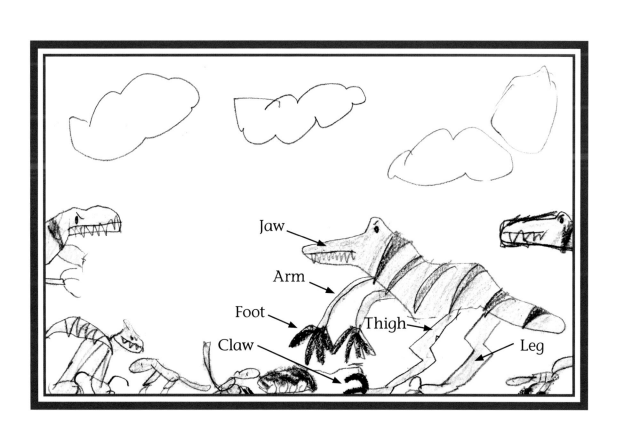

Massive Meat Eaters

T-Rex

by Sanampreet

Tyrannosaurus Rex, or T-Rex, was the King of the Dinosaurs. Rex means "king." It could grow to 20 feet tall. It was one of the biggest meat eaters scientists have ever studied. T-Rex had huge teeth that were constantly being replaced.

T-Rex Fact File

T-Rex:

- walked on two legs
- used its long, heavy tail to balance
- had small arms with clawed fingers
- had a very strong bite
- weighed eight tons
- lived in forest areas

Spinosaurus
by George

Spinosaurus was another huge meat eater. It was even bigger than T-Rex! Scientists think that Spinosaurus could swim. Its wide, flat feet and claws were good for swimming.

It probably spent lots of time in water, catching big fish like sharks to eat. Spinosarus had a big sail on its back. This helped protect it from other dinosaurs.

What Would Dinosaurs Eat Today?

by Victoria

Earth was very different when dinosaurs were here. Plants were different. Mammals were only very small. If plant-eating dinosaurs lived today, they could eat ferns, small plants, and grass. Meat-eating dinosaurs could eat small animals. They might eat big mammals like lions, too. They might even eat us! We would have to watch out!

Plant—eating dinosaurs   Meat—eating   dinosaurs

Where Would Dinosaurs Live Today?

Some dinosaurs were very big. They couldn't live in towns and cities. They could live in forests. Maybe herds of Apatosaurus would live in fields like cows. Maybe T-Rex would live in the rain forests of South America. Maybe Velociraptors would live in the deserts of Australia. It might be too cold for dinosaurs to exist at all. The Earth was hotter when dinosaurs were around.

Life would sure be different if dinosaurs lived today!